Portraits

Maía

Untimely Books

Untimely Books

untimelybooks.com
An imprint of Cosmos Cooperative
PO Box 3, Longmont, Colorado 80502
info@untimelybooks.com

Cover Art by Maía
Book design by Kayla Morelli

The text for this book is set in Plantagenet Cherokee. Italic and bold text is set in Source Serif Variable. Poem titles are set in Sacre Bleu MVB.

Publisher Cataloging-in-Publication Data

Names: Maía, 1944-, (Poet), author.

Title: Portraits / Maía.

Description: Longmont, CO : Untimely Books, 2023. | Summary: Portraits is a group of "poem-paintings" of human and more-than-human subjects whose lives and ways have inspired the poet. This volume includes homages to James Baldwin, Thomas Merton, Denise Levertov, Rachel Carson, Barry Lopez, Vincent van Gogh, and other notable humans, as well as sea sparrows, parrots, mockingbirds, and starling kin... mother ocean, old-man river, spruce groves and kelp... comb jellies, grey gulls, anemones, green crabs, whelks and periwinkles. Maía's intimate portraits show us how we can see these people and beings who belong to our world in a poetic new light.

Identifiers: LCCN 2023940078 | ISBN 9781961334014

Subjects: LCSH: American poetry -- 21st century. | LCGFT: Poetry. | BISAC: POETRY / American / General | POETRY / Women authors | POETRY / Subjects & Themes / Animals & Nature.

Classification: DDC 811.6

LC record available at https://lccn.loc.gov/2023940078

For Charlie

Contents

Finished, Baby

First heard your voice shimmer round the radio

cracking words like *justice* between your teeth, I could nearly

feel those enormous bruised eyes of yours

from magazine portraits, eyes that've seen, you said,

too many men die

       heard you, tender in the belly of a rant,

call and response, scalding illumination—

what does a white American singing Black spirituals

even think those words mean?!

       and all the time sadness

constricts your air—astonishing phrases

a long time coming, long time blowing out, luminous

rest—a drink of silence

       starting again *weary how weary...*

a short sharp laugh, a slap of hard logic on the tail

of smart-as-hell rejoinders, pouncing

on the least ignorance or arrogance out of the mouth

of the white female reporter interviewing you...

same one gifting you to us years later

over alternative airwaves, station KPFK, LA future-present

city of incendiary angels—you

in the ground by then, blazing spirit

      gone a long season

      & somehow I hear you

pacing your old room on Horatio Street, it's a truly hot summer &

Lady's *Strange Fruit* drifts in through your window, that song

all day & half the dark—Ma Rainy, too—scratched disk

spinning the table, the cosmos, mean needle

going so deep no end to it...

      & all the little children like grass

come twig come flowering bud come Mama an Daddy—well, I *walked*

and I walked till I wore out my shoes, can't walk long,

and yonder come the blues...

      & I heard you rest your mind

against your lover's hip, pleasure breaking you forever and ever

til you think you can't take more, and then it turns around

& you butterfly-stroke & you rise

exultant as Aphrodite...

…voice on the radio,
pain bending each word as you speak about straight white men
following you home, talking dirty, moaning into your shoulder,
begging—you could feel it—to be forgiven, shriven
by means of your Blackness…

    & after all that, what could you possibly say
to this world except *I'm finished with all that, baby—*
let the fireball fly!

Kentucky Woods

Thomas Merton

She was with you in winter her fragrance

before and behind you, her footprints tracked snow where you walked

for hours in the wake of the bobwhite's cry, falling silent,

and in springtime when the heron spied for God

on the little fishes, turning them to winged flesh—you turned

the whole world into her, your *Beloved*,

she might have wept for you who were made for solitude, word-lover

who could never drink deep enough *no-word*,

she might have laughed at your bad moods, the little scrapes

you got yourself into, bending the rules, she might have known

how you'd fall in love with a woman, in your ordinary frame

your fleshy soul, hands thick with the cutting and binding

of stalks, hauling water-buckets up the slope to the hermitage,

your hide-out under her wing, Our Lady of Carmel

hovering above, bright moon—and below, the luminous nape

of a perfect white mushroom arching from soil *always with you,*

no matter what, no matter how far you traveled

from home, Gethsemane, crescent of her face

turning toward your face, even in the dirty mirror of a Cuban hotel,

in the hollow eyes of a Calcutta beggar-girl, that glance

an arrow piercing your breast

and in the end when you traveled East, she was with you

in the gravity of your last reach

for the burning fan—

       whirr of quail dancing
               at the edge of Kentucky Woods

Mockingbird Night

Four-Hundred Tongues/Western Mockingbird

Silence, the simplest prayer, falls at dusk

when blue dark comes fast, and we sing what we hear,
   you and I, our last late repertoire—

and for a time, all is concord.

But soon our themes diverge, you gush on—
   wedding chants, boasts, jokes, even

parakeet and cockatiel mourning the other's
   distant company, back and forth

from separate cages—

harsh piercing furious you exult in every state
   of soul, love or torment, echoing note

for note, while I beg for the mercy of sleep.

Near dawn, heaven and the ground
    stunned in the crack! of thunder

then silence. That silence
    after the end and before the beginning—

storm, orgasm, concussion,
    surrender…

without any promise of rain.

Inside the shockwave
    inside my pulse, your green desire…

nothing can stop you
    canta y canta y canta para nadie

Speaking to the Mountain

Denise Levertov

I heard her—that charming whistle
between her teeth—as she spoke poetry, rocking

on the balls of her feet, at the mic on a platform
to give her small frame height—chin up, fists curled

at the small of her back—speaking to us
of the full moon's untamed blaze, flaunting the laws
of physics—luminous sphere passing whole

through slashing poplars, through the mesh
of window-screen, and over the sill into her kitchen—

wandering every cold dark room of the house,
coming to rest in the pit of her forehead, *pain*

like a vision between her eyes like sun
glancing off snow on Mt. Rainier in Spring.

2

Born Welsh-Russian-English, now Oregon's
rough green rain-catch *home*, the holy mountain

she declined to name in a hundred mornings,
in a hundred verses. She died in winter.

Breast cancer—*the women's plague*—
what have we learned since her leaving?

She said it's easier to love the cockroach in his small
brown habit, gnawing the wire of the world,

than to change our ways.

3

The nightingale was rushed to the royal physicians,
    her lungs folded shut like wings

and all their sulfur and all their radium
    couldn't save her.

Mountain, receive her.

Captive

Amazon Parrot

A breeze wakes me in the smoky gray
    before morning, wind chimes shattering space

as the world shifts toward daylight
    between the slats, and she murmurs

dissent—the neighbors' parrot on her rung—
    in the rattle of wind through the bars of her cage.

I'm alone in a strange room, listening to her soft
    whistle through the wall, falling

into a drowse, then roused by those
    tiny bells, questioning notes.

On frigid nights, I worry over her like a child,
    her small phrases trickling through the seam between

dream and dying, into the violet-blue
    inside my skull,

grateful for her translations
    of exile I can only guess at, grateful to lie for hours

in her little flares and flags and musical puzzlings
    addressed to the one who trapped her—

she might remember
    rivers dragging mist-scarves, red beacon of berries,

mosaic of leaves, light on water, her own wild kind
    lifting her into flight...

The Small Zone

Irina Ratushinskaya

Why do we say a garden
   must be larger than a single leaf?

Women of the Small Zone keep a secret garden—
   carrot chive turnip seeds smuggled in the seams
   of shirts, hems of jackets—
   shapely grains, precise botanic alphabet
   passed between prisoners—code
   intelligible to fingertips

Irina is the one who writes, bending
   over her forbidden poem, microscopic script,
   minute verses inscribed on strips of paper,
   four centimeters wide *rolled tight…*
   smaller than the little finger
   small enough to smuggle—
   seeds in poems out

Do you know what wealth is? A few words
   from a stranger, a few leaves of the goosefoot
   or crumbs of tobacco, bits of bread saved
   for somebody who's older or sicker
   or lonelier than you are

Small Zone women sow black stony soil
   around the well among concealing weeds
   Nothing is wasted—*every blade and every leaf*
   studied for its medicine—Dandelion
   Dillweed   Caraway   Clover

Irina conceives her minute poems
   composing all night on the cold Shizo floor,
   in the stink of the night bucket,
   warming herself with words, passing on
   a little heat to the next cell
   Seeds in   Poems out
   like the slow eccentric spiral of blood
   through the heart

Consolation happens like this—
   a nameless flower from the garden
   warmed against the breasts,
   slipped into Shizo where Irina
   wild-eyed with fever, murmurs
   to this flower, mother to child

      2

When the garden is found out
   the guards who have no green inside them
   destroy it, taking pleasure, taking care
   to sift the soil for every fugitive root

Hope is the everyday knife hidden
    in its everyday place. To lose it is perilous,
    to find it is to sleep on the tip
    of the blade

By Small Zone prisoners' sleight of hand,
    seeds are pulled from empty pockets,
    the little claw of chive takes hold,
    cleaving itself from stone
    and mineral, swelling, and sugaring
    Chive shoot homely as grass
    concealed from the guard's eye
    by resemblance to what is for him
    common and worthless—
    only the lover sees exact

Each detail carved in memory—
    red berries of the rowan at Barashevo,
    a woman, spellbound as she draws water,
    one leaf of yellow poplar spinning
    at the bottom of the well

Irina divides the harvest eleven times,
    reciting forbidden verses—
    sometimes only a mouthful, a single line
    from a poem for each woman,
    a single leaf passes around the table
    green eyelid bright against the tongue

3

Once under the big Russian night
    a river caught fire—A woman heard the cuckoo
    and counted its cries—How many years,
    little bird, are left to this Earth?

The Small Zone now is a strange museum,
    but somewhere—another cell, another country
    a prisoner remembers the wind—
    through the iron chink the same refrain
    of birches and fences—
    footprints in the long snow

And when they let Irina go
    she begins to write her poems

    one

        word

            for every page

Echo

Rachel Carson

At the edge of light in the rhythm
of the hammock, under a steady fall of ash

from Pittsburgh steel mills fourteen miles
away, over cottage and outhouse lit
by candle-stub, kerosene, in the choke
of coal drift dusting the pond and every
leaf, pea-vine, sheet, and nightgown
on the wash-line—you were born.

Through Springdale woods you spoke first
to the dawn—*hermit thrush! cardinal!*—
consulting the starlings' dark burble—ocean
wingbeat, coastal murmur in your ear
la mer calling you

blood-pulse, swinging arms, and legs
on long walks to school—grass-ripple
breath-rise wind-fall—never-seen-
or-heard *Atlantic*, liquid clamor rushing
to sudden silence—

2

All through the lunar month as the moon
waxes and wanes, so the moon-drawn
tides increase or decline...

as you, muse of fallen seaside sparrows,
gave your life away to those who needed you,
sustained your spirit in slender
crevices of time, ink moving your mind
over the sandy page

In the sea, nothing lives to itself

The great body of mother-ocean
circulates hormonal instructions altering the fate
of beings who haven't arrived yet, lives
touching lives distant in time

spruce groves and kelp, comb jellies, grey gulls,
anemones, green crabs, whelks and periwinkles,
flowering dunes, laughing women...

In the beginning... was the plankton

Before almost anyone you heard the largest
alarms that would be ours 50 years on—cold-loving
creatures shifting north, away from tainted,
warming waters—stone by stone, the ocean
taking back her ancient coasts.

We who live today can only wonder;
a rising sea could write a different history

3

And because you loved night and water-by-starlight,
you loved her, quiet woman reflecting your wild
or sacrificial seasons, withdrawals, restorations

wave after wave of love letters, then the long
wait between, dreaming her voice by the loud Atlantic
or at your hermit's desk in the company of oceanic
language, undulations of storm-light, she

the lee, seawall to your cross-winds—she, the land,
not famous Anemone Cave or Thunder Hole, but
an unnamed niche behind a living curtain
of greenery, sea-cove woman

pulling against publisher's deadlines—beach walks
with your orphaned grandnephew, with friends...
and those lost woods on the Maine coast
you ached to snatch from developers...

Instead, your gift to Earth, to generations, *Silent Spring,*
book of revelations—biocides and corporate lies—
grave warning delivered to Congress while you were barely
able to stand after radical mastectomy and radiation...

already leaving us—*returning*
to water air wind rock wing-back ash at dawn—*almost*
physical immortality

receding to our flat blue future
in the Anthropocene, firm horizon melting
to mirage, time foreshortening
your rosaries of tentacle and carapace

Sea Around Us, Edge of the Sea,
Under the Sea Wind

beyond our hearing range, the plover's warble,
seaside sparrow's diminished whistle,
leap-tide neap-song

—our end
in our beginning

echo obeyed in childhood before you
ever heard it—echo
      from fiery sea-bed—cliff-edge
where terra firma whirls
         to star and foam

and time stops and you wander and everything
worth saying is being said by the sea

Horizon

Barry Lopez

It was the very last Sunday of a dry
Southern California December, La Niña winter
like your childhood and mine.

The last hour of sundown held me in the cold garden.
Two voices rang out—amphibian poets
silent since March—and I understood:

all year they listen for the hum
of leaves that says *rain, near future tense,*
the curtain already falling long before we know it.

And listening, I'm released to head home
with the crows, to catch the dark news.

Barry Lopez died Christmas Day...
He was seventy-five.

~

Morning. Leaves shiver under drops—
rain, present tense, whole notes, slow as grieving.
I'll remember this, I'll compare

the rhythm of this late December rain
to *patience.* Your words held now
between the lips of silence.

2

All things are made by the wind. By water.

The boy you were and the man,
eye of water bird, dry branch, desert crystal—
light music, masterpiece of polar ice—

numinous interiors *real*
as texture and color, as rock wolf cloud fire…

The anthropologist, Alan Walker, once said to you
with his hands on the smooth skull
of an australopithecine, *Barry, I can't prove this*
but I believe we sang before we spoke.

3

30 years to write *Horizon*, your last book.

Afterward, you longed to travel
down enough to touch the gouged Pacific basin,
birth scar where Moon broke out of Earth.

You quit that manuscript so many times,
came begging to the Mackenzie where beavers built
and re-built after storms and wildfire…

where a wand of alder, an ash stick,
nudged your hand—you got the message,
and kept on writing.

You always took the long way around.

~

Of time and human existence, you said
it needs to be redreamed.

At hospice, McKenzie twigs arrived on a current
of human hands—those who knew you, knew
alder, willow, ash, the beavers' labor

riverine refuge—your bed, surrounded
by friends, by trees who remember
rain and time before words,

time and rain—after.

Hermes, Old Man

Will Inman

The old man talks to the river
the river that runs through the desert and disappears,
talks to the river like bees talk to nectar,
talks to rocks, to the red dust
chanting *O the river*

talks to whirlwinds, to devils peeled loose
from burnt trees, talks them down
and blesses them, down from the scorched
apricot, the one in his orchard
that refuses to bear—he takes hold
of a numb blue bud and breathes on it,
sends made-up words into it

talks to his food while he cooks,
to the spider in the stove, to moth wings
crumbling into his soup
telling himself stories, *once there was
a boy who stole fruit but
could not eat*

Neighbors roll their eyes.
He's the one with no woman,
the one holed up in a knocked-in trailer
on the edge of the great Sonora
tending a garden of hollyhocks, every shade
of the rainbow even black—
which he loves best—damp velvet
nap of the bumblebee

The old man talks to the river
goes down to wash himself, remembers
his mother blind and mute in the hospital bed—
how he stood there and suddenly knew
death makes you thirsty
fed her drops from a spoon—
she smiled in her coma and the bones
of his skull widened

He says this world is fire
giving birth to water, that's why he kneels
in the river where the sun licks
the sacred bowl of the hips

stripped naked

as the one who lives there

drowned and immortal, the god

who grasped him once, pulled him down

and kissed him on the mouth

At One with Everything

Little Brown Bat

Tonight, I asked the dusk to let me see you

one more time—none of your kind found here

for years now. Every blue sundown I'm looking for

your erratic rhythm, dip, and dive in crepuscular

time so out of favor now—only

mosquito's pleased with this upsidedown

day-for-night world where you are

hidden at one with everything.

They don't know what they do

when they curse you *black as night*, you

who inspire last-ditch prayers

or fear, when you show your sphinx-face

dusted with starlight, shadow-imp, sprite

less graceful than owl, less agile

than swallow, furred mammal on the wing

devouring your weight in insects every night,

at dawn nursing your pup from teats

as women do. Mother of tourmaline, your

color born of darkness, inaudible mantra,

white violet, all things most rare—*there*—

do my eyes invent your flight across this garden?

And if it's you, light-fleeing mouse-ear,

are you leaving us—or returning?

Mirrors of Agnès

"If we opened people up, we'd find landscape.
If we opened me up, we'd find beaches."

Agnès Varda, *The Beaches of Agnès*

Maybe cloud music and rain-light tutored you,
girl-child, playing ball up and down Rue de l'Aurore
without any look-out to the sea, stranded
on narrow, steep-sided streets, all doors
opening straight into traffic, cobblestones
where somehow you caught the opal
and aquamarine fever of saltwater
in the mirror at the back of your eye—
later on, that vision magnified, in star-facing
waters and crystals of sand.

In war-broken Paris, *streets were cold and dark,*
you were galvanized by sunlight pulsing on the Seine's
sinuous bright artery flowing under lindens
and horse chestnuts, steeples, and bridges, you
and that river listening for the sea.

Grown woman, still elfin in Buster Brown
cut, often inaudible, tongue-tied vagabond,
French-Greek sailor-girl, alone, ashore

in loose clothes, oversize shawls, disguising
the sly oceanic bones of your body's
contradictory intelligence—ageless,
restless, tentacular—hunting runes
veined with light. Indecipherable poetics.
Even for poets who sink lines
to the bottom of language.

~~~

Little by little your *self-strange* eye uncovered
her kin: the comic duende of alley cats
and accidents. Cracks and stains, ideograms
cross-hatching a ceiling. A castoff tribe
of withered spuds with poison hearts
and Medusa frizz. Even that hunched Ancient
floating ahead of you—yes, even young
you foreshadowed her, trailing
your seaweed scarves...

For you, it was solitude as still-life: seabird's egg
balanced on an elegant bed
of sea grass—*complete*. Until the day you fell
under the spell of the cello in Jacques' voice—
tender-eyed paramour, like you he adored
in perpetual motion, hungry for life
even after the AIDS diagnosis,
~~~

the two of you, like mirrors flashing
alternate versions of one another—apart
or side by side—until the hour
his breath stopped.

   ~~~

And so you return to the music of beaches,
filming your late self-portraits along the strand,
planting a dream-forest of mismatched mirrors—
framed or bare or asymmetrical, minuscule
or grand—every one of them looking
straight into the tidal return, your earliest visions
rushing to meet you again in old age...

Agnès studying Agnès, your camera a gliding
pelican over contours, textures of your body's
worn sea rock, twisting veins, well-traveled
coastlines, that avian lens-eye circling

swooping in flight, salvaging ghost-particles,
centrifugal art of your calling, following
rhythms of water and light and time—
that oldest *magic*—still
turning the blackest grief of the Sea
to Seine blue.
   ~~~

Muse of One-Breasted Women

Deena Metzger

I asked for a poem—it came to me
in the form of a pelican, a large ungainly
male, adorned in mating colors, bard
of elbows and prehistoric umbrellas

I asked for the sea, she showed me
a woman on her side, one breast
missing. She brought me a mirror
All mirrors distort

The face in the waves,
is it mine? She gave me salt
to clean the wound, gave me thread
Do your own mending, she said

I asked for music. What bait
could lure her? Now and then a new word—
the tinkling of a silver earring
as I stroll into the dunes

In her heart, a great crowd—
she's weary of poets pursuing,
pen in hand. I don't blame her,
too many lovers can be

a torment. I asked for the sea
she showed me a woman,
breast missing, chest tattooed
with the wings of birds.

I have passed through fire—
blackened, stripped, discarded
all my glistening chambers,
my seed pearl linings...

Afterward, pain, the surgeon told her,
would be brilliant but small
Distant as Spica in the Virgin's hip.
He lied, she said.

Tonight I stitched her a cap
of feathers, the design celestial,
repeating, finely ordered
as the oblong clouds of Georgia O'Keeffe.

Tonight, I tried the cap
on my own head—and I slept, my arms
around the Dark, rocking me
out to deep water, the salt waves...

She led me down, down.
Cry your own tears, she said.

The Natural Selection of Desire

Black-chinned Hummingbird

because the female hummingbird desires
jade-becoming-turquoise

because the bee sucks rosemary flowers
blue aromatic breasts, her

many lovers, because freesia bulbs erect
rows of white buds along the arch

because the tongue of the fritillary
licks the eyelashes of passionflower

because wild buckwheat unfolds
her pleated clusters

because thyme creeps along the earth
ripe purple-green, because

nothing's more like blood-drops
than petals of scarlet geranium

because the heat of the sun glistens
poppy silk, the capsule sweats

bitter opium, and the squash blossom
withers when pistil tastes pollen

and the green fruits clasped in the calyx,
and the fig draws the fig wasp

inside, to hide her eggs in the starry
pouch, and the beetle tumbles

into the wide yellow heart
of the blooming cucumber, because

the sparrow flies with a burdock seed
tucked into her feathers

and the burr of the spike weed travels
on the woman's sandal as she

wades through coyote-bush fluff
like the stuffing of an ancient couch

left out in the field where they first
made love because he saved

the whisk-broom seeds of marigold
in a tiny glassine envelope, she

and his sister scattered them
the summer he died—he keeps on

blazing at the tail-end of August
because the male hummingbird sheens

and shoots earthward—a comet
from the Sky of the female

Fire

"I feel a fire in myself which I cannot allow to die."

Vincent van Gogh

They lowered him
two thousand feet into the bowels
of earth—stunned dust
in a slow perpetual churn

Anchorite miners
scraping in rows by watery lanterns,
pick-blows aimed by touch
by intuition

Coughing ash and granite,
he rode up again, could never
say why he came to love
the underground, the buried

burnt gleam of Rembrandt
over the miners' rough hands

2

Christ of the Mineshaft, the colliers
called him Evangelist of black-earth country
Belgium   The Borinage   The black day
Twelve hours chipping the coal-face

He gave away his bed, his shoes, slept
in the hayrick, sewed shirts from sacking, fed
milk to the barn cat—for himself
water and bread   He rose

with the miners before the sulfur sun
The grey sun dragged him back
at shift's end, light snuffed
in the heath, the stars'

anthracite burning past all reach
past hunger and the miners' shuffling dance
Between the fume and the dust
give us our daily breath

say us grace, slumped round the table,
ashy tubers dug from frozen ground, roasted
in coal slash, the blood-heat
melting snow around each hut

3

Noon   Too many cigarettes   Hawking
and squinting over the rattling page
With a nub of charcoal, he'd catch the miners
streaming up the pit like termites

after water—the boil of gossip and grim jokes
of those who go down every day to death
Au Charbonnage, black beer and a rest,
a penny candle for the wounds of Jesus

At day's end he sketched them,
bent as though against tremendous wind,
coal-sacks humped on spines, strapped
over foreheads, one of the women

swinging a lantern over the path
at dusk, every tree a torso
twisting in the wood   In his mind, a letter
scribbling itself, never sent, *Dear*

Theo… I find God even in the stench
of piss against the barn where some beggar
has rested a moment and dragged
farther on   And in the flesh

of the blackened potato
when the skin is pierced and the hot mist
touches the cheeks and the throat moistens
and one faints with pleasure

   4

Shorn grass, the short summer laid down
in fat over bone   Pollen, the tongues
of cold flowers, rain silvering
the leaf   Vincent's rapture bent

to the stalks, the shadow of his head
over the glory of the wheat,
his blue eye on the bloody feather
floating from the thorn hedge—summer

blackening, the heath tearing with snow
Smoke roaring up the mineshaft

   5

All night, shouts and curses
church bells tolling and the hammering
of caskets, bed sheets stripped
and torn for bandages

Bodies hauled up in pony carts
under the scorched wind   He couldn't recall
the flash in the pit, only
a young man's boot

dangling against his thigh
as he carried him out of the mine
His eyes shied away from the miners
who had witnessed him

speaking of mercy   How could he say
to them now *there is no mercy* because
of a boy's boot, the smallest part
of the conflagration, dropped lantern

catching a pantleg, crawling flesh
Delirium—every word he ever spoke
betraying him   Like a burden of coal,
he laid the boy in the road

slashed boot-leather from the ankle,
knowing the whole leg would have to go
Around him, men hurried down again
refusing to abandon the mine

He received the boy's breath,
the faithful blood still beating
under the kneecap, shooting down
the shin to the hot sole

of the foot, membranes peeling back
to bone white as birch twigs   Vincent's lungs
craving air, a shirtsleeve against
his lips to stop a scream

That night, the miners said you could hear
the preacher weeping in the barn,
in the hay-breath of the cows
A madman, they said   Or a saint

In the morning, eyelids seamed
with coal dust, it was useless to bathe
Air, earth, water—smoked
and stained   Only fire pure

6

The Pastorage, they called him back,
saying, son, our Lord does not require us
to go about in rags, filthy as miners—you insult,
don't you see, the dignity of our profession

In failed sermons, in the scandal of passion
his visions began—gold weft, the fire
of hay-stems rustling and shining
and the comical rumbling

bellies of the beasts, the glister
of their sorrowful eyes   His own eyes
in a chip of mirror, each a different blue
And the muscular tenderness

of clouds, crosshatch of winter, nude
cast in ice, voluptuous snow dune

7

Maybe his woman appeared to him then—
pregnant with a stranger's child,
the cradle rocking, rocking, starry night

She shaves his head, the razor stropped
and foamed, relieving the lice-prick
behind his ears, the search

that never lets him rest   She laughs
He admonishes her to love
even lice snapped between the nails

Because God has passed through all flesh
and death to reach us, how can we
refuse?   Maybe she kissed him

and laid her hands on his nakedness
maybe she showed him the peacock
in the shaft of light, showed him

the sea at Les Saintes Maries,
let him draw her
by the sallow light of the sun—

and he saw then he was nobody's
preacher, driven from the word
to love God's body

in the bowed back of the miner,
the **no** and the **never**—until—
keeping his hand to the flame,

he began to paint the sky

Notes on the Poems, and Selected Resources

Finished, Baby (James Baldwin, 1924–1987)

Epigraph: from "Freaks and the American Ideal of Manhood", *Playboy*, January, 1985

I walked and I walked—from lyrics by Ma Rainey, "Walking Blues", Ma Rainy: Complete Recorded Works In Chronological Order Vol. 1, Document Records, 1924

This use of "baby" was Baldwin's habit of speaking, though the phrase is not a quote.

Resources:

James Baldwin: Collected Essays, Edited by Toni Morrison, (Library of America, 842 pp, 1998) includes "The Fire Next Time", "Notes of a Native Son", "Nobody Knows My Name", and many others

James Baldwin, The Cross of Redemption: Uncollected Writings, ed. Randall Kenan, Pantheon, 2010

James Baldwin: Living in Fire, (biography) by Bill V. Mullen, Pluto Press, London, 2019

I Am Not Your Negro, (film) dir. Raoul Peck, 2016, Magnolia Pictures/ Amazon Studios

Kentucky Woods (Thomas Merton, 1915–1968)

In the end… while on his Asian journey, staying in Bangkok, still wet from a hotel shower, he was electrocuted while reaching for an electric fan

Resources:

See especially Merton's seven-volume personal journals, *Harper One*, 2009

And the autobiography, *The Seven Story Mountain*, Harcourt Brace, first edition, 1949

Mockingbird Night (Northern or Western Mockingbird)

The Tsalagi (Aniyvwiya) or Cherokee called this native, Southeastern Cherokee-territory singer, "Four Hundred Tongues" long before a later variety began to spread north and west, now ranging from Canada to upper Mexico; though both sexes sing, it is the male who keeps it up all hours of the night, beginning in early Spring, weaving his own musical verses between short repeating phrases lifted from the natural and human world of sound.

Species: *Mimus polyglottos*

Speaking To The Mountain (Denise Levertov, 1923–1997)

Resources:

Collected Poems, ed. P. Lacey; A. D. Dewey; E. Boland. New Directions, 2013

A Poet's Revolution: The Life of Denise Levertov (biography) by Donna K. Hollenberg, Univ. of CA Press, 2013

Captive (Amazon parrot)

Species: Scarlet-lored Amazon parrot, *Amazona autumnalis*

The Small Zone (Irina Ratushinskaya, 1954–2017)

The Small Zone: a women's sector which held eleven inmates, inside a
larger Russian prison

Shizo: punishment cell, solitary (an acronym for *"shtrafnoy izolator"*)

Italicized phrases from *Grey Is The Color of Hope*, by Irina
Ratushinskaya, Sceptre, 1988

Echo (Rachel Carson, 1907–1964)

all through the lunar months—from *Edge of the Sea* (cited below)

the muse of fallen seaside sparrows—adapted from "the God of fallen
sparrows" in Rachel Carson's field notes

In the sea nothing lives to itself... In the beginning... we who live today...
—from *Edge Of The Sea*

the woman—refers to Dorothy Freeman (see *Always Rachel*, cited below)

almost physical immortality—an insight omnipresent in her work

(everything) *worth saying is being said by the sea* is my adaptation of
"all that was worth saying was being said by the sea"—in *Lost Woods*
(cited below)

Resources:

Lost Woods: Found Writings of Rachel Carson by Linda Lear, Beacon
Press, 1999

Always Rachel: The Letters of Rachel Carson and Dorothy Freeman, 1952-
1964, Edited/Intro by Linda Lear, first edition, 1998, Beacon Press

*The Sea Around Us, The Edge of The Sea, Under The Sea Wind (New
American Library/Mentor paperbacks, 1954)*: Carson's poetic
trilogy balancing imaginative and empirical experience with
scientific fact; not much read now compared to *Silent Spring* (1962,
Houghton-Mifflin)

Horizon (Barry Lopez, 1945–2020)

Resources:

See especially, *Lopez's Horizon*, 2020, Vintage, London; *Arctic Dreams: Imagination and Desire in a Northern Landscape*, 2001, Vintage, New York; *Light Action In The Caribbean* (stories), 2000, Knopf; *Giving Birth To Thunder, Sleeping With His Daughter: Coyote Builds North America*, 2001, Harper Perennial

Terry Gross' interview with Lopez (recorded much earlier, aired 2021), https://npr.org/2021/01/954833226/remembering-nature-writer-barry-lopez

Hermes, Old Man (Will Inman, 1923–2009)

The old man talks to the river / the river that runs through the desert… Will was a neo-Whitmanian Arizona poet… also a friend/correspondent of mine.

Resources: https://en.wikipedia.org/wiki/Will_Inman_(poet)

At One With Everything (Little Brown Bat)

Title: from a line by Thomas Merton

Species: *Myotis lucifugus*, endangered in some regions

Mirrors of Agnès (Agnès Varda, 1928–2019)

Agnès (AN-yes) Varda

If we opened people up… and the streets were cold and dark—A. Varda

self-strange: "self-strange to the point of innocence": from quote by Hèléne Cixous, in *Woman, Native, Other: Writing, Postcoloniality and Feminism* by Trinh T. Minh-Ha, 1989, Indiana University Press

Resources: See especially her films: *Black Panthers* (1968); *The Gleaners and I* (2000); *The Beaches of Agnès* (2008); *Faces Places* (2017); and her last, *Varda par Agnès* (2019)

Muse of One-Breasted Women

(Deena Metzger, 1936–)

Title/poem inspired by Deena, a long-time friend, and also the woman on a famous photo/poster (circulated especially by and among feminists since the 70s): her arms raised over her head, we see the scar where one of her breasts used to be, tattooed with leaves and a bird. Long ago, when I tried to post this image online, it was removed more than once—because of her nakedness

Resources: See her online blogs/essays, e.g., "The Language of Restoration" via substack.com, 2023

A few of her books: *La Negra y Blanca: Fugue and Commentary* (novel), 2011, Hand to Hand; *Ruin and Beauty: New and Selected Poems*, 2009, Red Hen Press; and (non-fiction) *Writing for Your Life: A Guide and Companion to the Inner Worlds*, 1992, HarperOne

The Natural Selection of Desire

(Black-chinned hummingbird)

Species: *Archilochus alexandri*

F i r e (Vincent van Gogh, 1853–1890)

Epigraph adapted from Letter #155 to Theo van Gogh: "Someone has a great fire in his soul and nobody ever comes to warm themselves at it… now what are we to do, (but) keep this fire alive inside…" original now at the van Gogh museum, Amsterdam

Resources: See *Letters to Theo* (several editions and translations). Biographical films, especially, *Loving Vincent* (2017) the world's first oil-painted, animated life-story told through 120 of his most well-known works and the characters/places they depict. (For more see lovingvincent.com)

Acknowledgements

"Captive," and "At One With Everything" (under the title "Prayer"), appeared in *Cholla Needles Journal #21* (2017)

"Echo" (2020) and "Horizon" (2021) appeared in the eco-political online-journal, *Resilience* (.org)

"One-Breasted Muse," in an earlier version, was published in the journal, *Solo II* (2006)

"Natural History of Desire," slightly altered, appeared in *Cholla Needles, #25* (2018)

Thank You

First and last, to all my relations—human and more than human.

Special Thanks to *Marco V Morelli* and *Kayla Morelli* who co-founded Cosmos Co-op, an online community of artistic and philosophical co-conspirators whose publishing imprint is Untimely Books.

And to *Douglas Duff* for his reading and comments on the finished poems.

Much gratitude to *Geoffreyjen Edwards*, *Andrea van de Loo*, *Michael Stumpf*, *Doug* and *Marco*, for "Labyrinth", a two-hour phone-based discussion group during which, over the course of more than a year, we read aloud together and discussed my speculative fiction, "cli-fi" novel, *See You In Our Dreams*. It was during several of these SYIOD salon-like meetings that the idea for *Portraits* arose.

Cover design for *Portraits* was an active collaboration among three of us, *Kayla*, *Marco* and myself. The cover image itself is my watercolor (titled "Fire"). Technical design work and elegance thereof is entirely thanks to *Kayla*.

And to *Emily Byrne* for her proofreading and bibliographic research.

Warm thanks to those who read and responded to some of these poems at various stages of revision: *Cynthia Anderson*, *Mary Kay Rummel*, and *Christian McEwen*.

And to *Dennis Rivers* for various kinds of help along the way.

—Maía, 2023

About the Author

Maía was born, raised, lives and writes on Southern California (Coastal Chumash) land. Previously published books of poetry: ***A Woman Green As The Sea*** (1991, Pieces of the Moon); ***SpiritLife of Birds*** (2012, Askew); ***Postcards from Jackson*** (2018, Cholla Needles Press). Also, a novel (speculative fiction): ***See You In Our Dreams*** (2020, Karuna Books and EcoVista Climate Justice Press).

In the works: ***Ancestors***—lyric and prose poetry inspired by her Eastern Clan Tsalagi (Cherokee) grandmothers and others, (artwork by her son, Tiadashi—TEE-uh DASS-see—derived from the transliterated Cherokee word for mountain lion—aka Dan Molina); ***Portraits II*** (Frida Kahlo, Pablo Neruda, et al—y La Familia de Las Plantas); and a new edition of ***See You In Our Dreams*** (Untimely Books).

Feedback/questions welcome: Maia@impulse.net

About Untimely Books

Untimely Books is an independent publisher of literary works that illumine the mind, question the contemporary, and reimagine horizons of thought, feeling, and action for a planetary age. As an imprint of Cosmos Cooperative (a creative community and member-owned publishing platform) and Metapsychosis (a journal of consciousness, literature, and art), Untimely Books serves as a conduit for diverse forms of writing by Cosmos members, including original works of fiction, poetry, philosophy, essays, memoir, and genre-fluid literature.

untimelybooks.com